The New K

The focus in this book is on the graphemes

ew, ue, igh

new   screwed

blue

alright   tight

Kevin and Wellington were upset.

Their kennel had gone. The rain had

taken it away. Where was their

kennel?

The two sad-looking dogs went to

the corner of the garden wall. They

looked all around the farmyard for

their kennel.

They saw it. Wow! It was down by the main gate to the farmyard. The gate had stopped it from being swept away down the road.

Kevin and Wellington ran to the main gate. They inspected their kennel from every side. It was alright. It was not broken!

Farmer Robert went to look at it too. The kennel was alright. So he put a rope round it and pulled it tight with the tractor.

Then he dragged the kennel across

the farmyard. Crunch! Crack! Oh no!

The back wall got stuck on a stone.

Oh no! The wood split.

Oh no! The sides came away from the back. The roof came off. The whole kennel collapsed in a heap in the middle of the farmyard.

Kevin and Wellington were upset
again. But Farmer Robert drove into
town and he came back with a
trailer full of new wood.

He fixed some pieces of wood to the old kennel floor. Then he screwed new sides to the wood. He fixed a new roof to the top.

He painted the kennel blue like the old one. Kevin and Wellington were happy. Their new kennel would not float away like the old one.

Vowel graphemes

ai/ay/a-e:	rain main trailer painted away taken gate came
ee/ea:	heap
y/i-e/igh:	by sides like alright tight
oa/o-e/o:	road float rope broken drove whole stone old
ue/ew:	blue new screwed
oo:	roof too
oo:	look wood sad-looking looked
ow/ou:	down town wow around
or:	for corner floor
ar:	garden farmyard Farmer
er:	corner Farmer Robert trailer
aw:	saw

INTRODUCTION

The restoration of the Kennet & Avon Canal is a great success story.

These days, the canal is widely enjoyed by canoeists, walkers, cyclists, anglers and holidaymakers and, in addition to these daily visitors, many people have chosen to make their homes here.

But it was not always like this. Two hundred years ago it was an essential means of transporting heavy goods and was busy with industrial traffic. Then, after the initial boom years, competition meant the canal fell into disrepair, and would have easily disappeared altogether if it wasn't for a group of dedicated enthusiasts who for many years have persevered with the revival of the old waterway.

England contrasting between tranquil tree-lined canal and open countryside, to the bustle of built-up areas of towns and cities. But even in more urban areas, the scene is a very different one from the industry of the early days.

Thanks to the Kennet and Avon Canal Trust new life has been breathed into it and different ways of using it have been found. And, although a piece of our cultural heritage, it continues to enhance our modern lives every day.

The canal connects Bristol to London.

Moorings

1

BUILDING THE CANAL

The Kennet & Avon Canal is made up of three parts. From Bristol to Bath, it follows the course of the River Avon and from Newbury to Reading, the course of the River Kennet. Both these rivers were made navigable in the 1700s. Later, the two rivers were joined by a 57 mile specially dug channel and the three parts were united under the Kennet & Avon Canal Company.

It was clear that connecting the two rivers would create a valuable link between the sea ports of Bristol and London. Heavy goods such as coal and stone could be transported inland instead of being shipped around the south coast, which would not only be less hazardous but also

Two rivers were joined by a purpose built channel.

save both time and money.

Although the need was recognised as early as Elizabethan times, it wasn't until the late 1700s that a serious proposal was put forward.

The first survey suggested a course that ran through the towns of Bradford-on-Avon, Melksham, Lacock, Chippenham, Calne and Marlborough before reaching Hungerford.

Because there were doubts over the water supply, another survey was carried out, this time by John Rennie. He was a skilled engineer, but did not have much

experience in canal construction at that time. He concluded that it would be preferable for the route to take a more southerly course and pass through Trowbridge, Devizes and Pewsey because it would reduce the construction time and be less expensive.

This was agreed upon and the money was raised by shareholders only too willing to invest in the new canal mania that was beginning to sweep the country.

Work started in 1794 with the navigators, or navvies for short, having been recruited from local farms. They used picks and shovels to dig the channel and wooden wheelbarrows to remove the earth. The ditch was then lined with clay to make it watertight. Different gangs started work on

John Rennie

different parts allowing some sections to be finished and in use before the whole was completed.

The terrain challenged Rennie to come up with major new ideas to overcome specific difficulties. Aqueducts, tunnels, lock flights and bridges all had to be designed, and many of the techniques developed during this time now form the basic principles of modern civil engineering.

Different types of bridges were essential to allow the world around the canal to continue, but Rennie didn't just design them to be useful, he made them beautiful. The stone and brick bridges' curved lines gave them extra strength as well as being aesthetically pleasing.

A close look at the stonework

Caen Hill Locks

Techniques developed to build the canal form the basis of modern civil engineering.

Swing Bridge

on the bridges and aqueducts will reveal many masons' marks. Some of these were carved at the quarry and used to identify where the stone should be positioned. Others were the signature marks of a particular mason which helped the master mason to see who was responsible for each job.

The wooden swing bridges, used mainly for pedestrian traffic, were made with one of Rennie's other inventions, the ball race. The pivot point of the bridge sits on two metal ring plates with ball bearings sandwiched between. This reduces the friction allowing the bridge to be effortlessly swung to the bank side when a boat needs to pass.

The middle section of the canal required eighty-one pound

The Caen Hill locks were the last part to be completed.

A ball-race is a ring-shaped groove in which metal balls move to reduce friction.

locks to be built, the last of these to be completed was the long series of locks on Caen Hill. While they worked on these, the canal operated in two halves. To enable goods to pass between the two, a horse-drawn tramway was built next to the line of the canal between Foxhangers and Devizes. Cargoes were unloaded into wagons and hauled by horses, then loaded into waiting boats to continue the journey.

The lock flight was finally finished and the canal was officially opened in 1810, sixteen years after it was started. The completed waterway was eighty-seven miles long with 106 locks and cost the incredible sum of one million pounds.

TRADE AND INDUSTRY

The introduction of the canal network led to a period of economic growth that had never been seen before. This was an exciting time in the early stage of the Industrial Revolution. Heavy goods such as coal and stone could be transported inland in large quantities, and having a good supply of fuel and building materials created many opportunities that were previously impossible.

Industries of all kinds such as sawmills, ironworks, fertiliser plants and factories grew up alongside the canal. Wharves were built where raw materials and finished goods were transferred to and from boats usually with the help of a small crane. Some wharves were owned by the K&A Canal Company, while others were privately owned.

They were very busy places for they were the industrial centres of their day where tradesmen, essential for the day to day running of the canal, quickly established themselves.

Carpenters were needed for boatbuilding; blacksmiths for shoeing horses; and waggoners made a living delivering goods from the wharves to the

surrounding areas. With so much activity, it was only natural that breweries, general stores and other services, needed to satisfy the workers, also thrived alongside.

In total, there were as many as 120 wharves with eighteen in Newbury, nineteen in Bath and even Devizes had as many as seven at one stage.

The K&A Canal Company had a duty to their shareholders to make money so in addition to the income from their wharves; they also charged tolls for using the canal. These were calculated by

Pewsey Wharf

5

the weight of goods carried per mile travelled. There were four rates for different types of cargo. Un-worked heavy items such as coal and stone had the lowest rates while manufactured and highly finished goods were charged at higher levels.

It was the toll-collectors' job to verify the cargo and gauge its weight. It was done using a gauging device which judged how low a boat sat in the water. Each craft was different so before it was licensed to use the canal, it was measured empty in a specially constructed gauging dock and

An unusual cargo of two thousand leeches was carried from London to Bath.

Many wharves had wooden cranes to help with the transfer of goods.

then again with each additional ¼ ton weight. The results were recorded on a chart and copies were distributed to all the tollhouses.

Coal was important for most industries and so was probably the most common cargo. It came from coalfields in Bristol and south Wales in the early days and then later from Somerset via the Somerset Coal Canal which joined near Bath.

The canal prospered from 1810 to 1841 until the introduction of the railway meant there was direct competition.

Burbage Wharf

World War II Bollards

DECLINE

The railway drastically cut the journey time from Bristol to London. After over 30 years of success, the K&A Canal Company faced difficulties.

They tried to compete by decreasing tolls and reducing maintenance costs, but in the end it was futile. The difference in speed meant more and more businesses began to choose to use rail.

At Parliament's suggestion, the K&A Canal Company was offered to the Great Western Railway in 1852 on condition they maintain it in a navigable condition. Although a legally binding agreement, it was not in their interests to spend money on something that was not profitable and inevitably it was neglected.

After the First World War, it was in a poor state and GWR proposed to close it altogether, but there was still some strong opposition. This, coupled with the costs of infilling, meant the idea was shelved.

During the Second World War, it was noted that the canal would be effective in stopping tanks moving north in the event of an invasion. The defences were strengthened by narrowing the road bridges with concrete bollards and pillboxes were built at regular intervals. Many of these guard posts are still preserved today.

But the deterioration continued and by 1950 large stretches were derelict. Most of the locks were rotten, the pumping stations were abandoned and the canal lining was not watertight. The bridges and aqueducts so painstakingly built were crumbling and overgrown.

Old Lock Gate

RESTORATION

During the 1950s, the canal was almost impossible to use, but people who lived in its vicinity seemed to have a close attachment to it. So when a group of enthusiasts put forward a plan to restore it for leisure pursuits, they were met with overwhelming support from the community. This dedicated group went on to form the Kennet & Avon Canal Trust in 1962. With the support of British Waterways, they raised money and organised the many volunteers who came forward to help.

The restoration unintentionally followed a similar pattern to the construction, with different sections being finished and used before the whole was completed. Work started by clearing the lock pounds of weed, rubbish and sediment. As money became available, more expensive and complex projects were tackled. Rotten lock gates were gradually replaced and leaking clay linings repaired.

By the 1970s, both the water-powered pumping station at Claverton and the steam-operated one at Crofton had been acquired and restored to their fully working states. They were opened to the public to raise money and thousands of people visited. But the income from boat moorings and entrance tickets were not enough on their own, so help was sought from local authorities and nearby businesses. The project gained momentum leaving only the Caen Hill Locks and the turf-sided locks between

The restoration was completed in 2003, although maintenance is ongoing.

Aldermaston and Newbury to do.

In 1990, it was again possible to travel by boat between Bristol and Reading, and as part of the celebrations, the Queen passed through Lock 43 of the Caen Hill flight.

Although functioning, the restoration was far from complete. There were still long-standing structural problems within the Bath valley and the water supply was also a big issue.

A second major phase of restoration began after a successful bid for £25 million from the Heritage Lottery Fund. This enabled the embankments to be stabilised and electric pumps to be installed to recycle lock water along the length of the waterway. Despite the restoration being

declared finished in 2003 with a visit from Prince Charles, maintenance is an ongoing task. For example, lock gates need replacing approximately every twenty-five years and they cost on average £100,000, which means a continuous programme of renewal to spread the cost.

The canal has not just been restored to a moment in history but improved and developed with the latest technology to make it viable in today's world. In the spirit of John Rennie, who had embraced the latest innovations when building the canal, it has been brought up to date.

Restoration Work

BRISTOL TO BATH

This section follows the course of the River Avon. The tidal river had been used since medieval times as far as Bristol, but travelling to Bath by boat was not really possible until 1727 when John Hore created a series of six locks. The development was highly desirable as Bath was becoming a very fashionable spa town.

The river was home to as many as thirty brass and copper mills in the 1700s. Bristol's copper industry relied on these mills to produce a variety of products for export to the furthest reaches of the British Empire. The river was used to transport the ingots to the

mills where waterwheels powered the rollers and hammers to manipulate the brass into pans, bowls and vats.

There are several remains of the old mills that can be seen by the river between Hanham Lock (1) and Saltford. The Saltford mill is open to the public on specified weekends and is run by volunteers. At the height of its productivity, it had five waterwheels and four furnaces; one of each still remain.

The pub alongside the Saltford Lock (4) has a fireplace surround which is full of holes. It was a tradition that a newly promoted captain would make his mark by burning a hole in the wood with a red-hot poker. The lock itself was

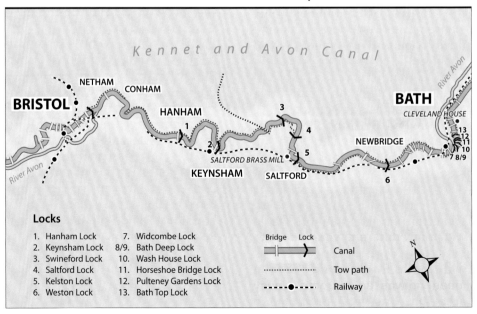

Locks

1. Hanham Lock	7. Widcombe Lock
2. Keynsham Lock	8/9. Bath Deep Lock
3. Swineford Lock	10. Wash House Lock
4. Saltford Lock	11. Horseshoe Bridge Lock
5. Kelston Lock	12. Pulteney Gardens Lock
6. Weston Lock	13. Bath Top Lock

Bridge Lock
Canal
Tow path
Railway

Kelston Brass Mill

the target of rebellious coal workers who were worried that the newly opened navigation would allow other collieries to transport coal to their customers. Kelston Brass Mill with its distinctive chimney can be seen opposite.

Leaving Saltford, the river travels through a valley with the Cotswold Hills rising on either side.

As the river enters Bath, many wharf-side warehouses can be seen; this was the main quayside with many different wharves lining the banks. The good connections with both Bristol and London meant it was an extremely busy area that was very important to the growth of the city in the Georgian period.

A major export was the famous honey-coloured Bath Stone. Ralph Allen, who owned the quarries, had his wharf on the river near to the canal's junction. This enabled the stone to be transported widely across the south of England and also via the sea ports as far afield as America and South Africa. The stone has been used for many grand buildings including Buckingham Palace in London.

The river was used for transport and power.

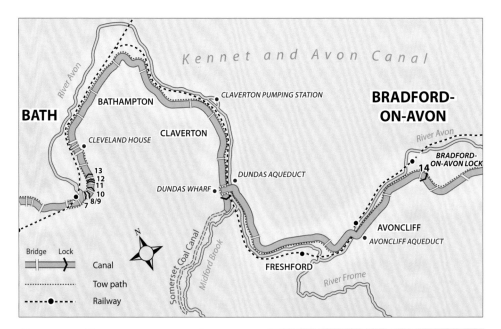

K e n n e t   a n d   A v o n   C a n a l

BATH

BATHAMPTON

CLAVERTON PUMPING STATION

BRADFORD-ON-AVON

CLEVELAND HOUSE

CLAVERTON

River Avon

BRADFORD-ON-AVON LOCK

14

13
12
11
10
8/9
7

DUNDAS AQUEDUCT

DUNDAS WHARF

AVONCLIFF

AVONCLIFF AQUEDUCT

Bridge   Lock

Canal

Tow path

Railway

N

FRESHFORD

River Frome

Somerset Coal Canal

Midford Brook

BATH TO BRADFORD-ON-AVON

The City of Bath lies in the Avon Valley and is surrounded by limestone hills where the renowned Bath Stone was quarried. The newly cut middle section of the waterway enabled the stone to be easily transported eastwards for the first time. The canal branches away just before Pulteney Weir, which is the navigable limit of the river, and climbs out of the valley using a series of six locks known as the

Pulteney Weir

Lock gates always point uphill. The design means they are forced shut when water tries to escape.

Widcombe Flight.

Originally, there were seven locks in the flight but Locks 8 and 9 were merged into one when the new road was built. Now called Bath Deep Lock, it is almost 6 metres (19ft) deep and is the second deepest in the country.

Alongside Horseshoe Bridge Lock (11) is an ornamental chimney that is all that remains of one of the two original pumping stations that stood here. They were designed to recycle the water from the bottom lock back to the top of the flight instead of it draining away into the river. The K&A Canal Company were found to be leaving the bottom gates of the lock open while pumping and so in effect were taking water directly from the river. They didn't have permission to do this and, after legal action from the local mill owners because it interfered with their water supply, were forced to close the pumping stations down.

The company's headquarters were in nearby Cleveland House. The three-storey Georgian building is interesting not only because it straddles the canal but also as it contains a hidden secret.

A close inspection of the tunnel's roof below will reveal a seemingly unremarkable rectangular hole. Although it only looks as if a brick is missing, it is in fact a shaft that connected to the cellar of the Company's offices above. Legend has it that it was for passing parcels or messages to the boats, but in fact it was a

Bath Deep Lock

refuse chute allowing waste from the basement kitchen to be deposited directly into the canal.

Junction of River Avon and Canal

That is, unless a boat was unfortunate enough to be passing underneath at the time!

The house sits on the edge of Sydney Gardens which is Bath's oldest park. The gardens were regularly visited by members of the royal family, and also by Jane Austen who lived locally for a while.

The course of the canal cuts the gardens in half and the two sides are joined by two ornamental ironwork bridges. These were built at the expense of the K&A Canal Company and, in addition, a hefty 2,000 guineas was paid to the landowners as compensation.

Bathampton is the home of

Cleveland House was originally called Canal House.

Cleveland House

Sydney Gardens

plasticine. The factory that made the modelling clay for distribution around the world was situated on the other side of the canal to the pub. Plasticine-filled barrels were still transported by narrow boat, even though the business was established after the railway.

The canal and the river, which are never very far from each other as they follow the contours of this scenic valley, meet again at Claverton where the water-powered pumping station has been fully restored. This unique piece of engineering was a very clever solution to feed water from the river to the canal 14½ metres (48ft) above. Renewable energy is now seen as fashionable but it was the only feasible solution in its day. The waterwheel is cylindrical

At full power, the waterwheel rotates five times a minute.

Claverton Pumping Station

in shape with a diameter of just over 5 metres (17ft) and has 48 wooden slats that are about 7 metres (24ft) long. The energy is transferred to cast iron rocking beams where each stroke lifts 230 litres (50 gallons) of water.

It was built by John Rennie and it worked continuously from 1813 until 1952 when it finally fell into disrepair.

As part of a project by the University of Bath and the Kennet & Avon Canal Trust, it was reopened in 1975 after being restored by a dedicated team of volunteers. Electric pumps have now taken over the day to day pumping, but there are days when it can still be seen in action and visitors are welcomed.

At Brassknocker Basin, the Somerset Coal Canal joins the Kennet & Avon. This was a highly profitable canal that was used to transport coal from the Somerset coalfields to the rest of the south of England. It is now largely filled

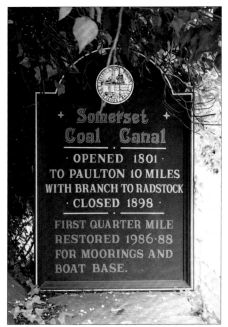

Dundas Aqueduct

in, but a short stretch from the junction has been restored and is used for moorings.

Just beyond, the canal leaps 137 metres (450ft) across the valley on the three-arch Dundas Aqueduct. It is one of the most well-known features on the Kennet & Avon and was named after Charles Dundas who was the first Chairman of the K&A Canal Company. An inscription on the south side commemorates his work.

It was designed by Rennie in a classical style to overcome the problem of the steep-sided valley. Built out of Bath Stone, the arches are beautifully proportioned. The main arch is 20 metres (65ft) wide and the decorative cornice extends over a metre (4ft) from the parapet. The stonework reveals many individual marks left by the masons who built it.

Three miles further on, the Avoncliffe Aqueduct brings the canal back across the valley. This was also designed by Rennie and included three arches. The central elliptical arch crosses the River Avon while the two smaller side arches cross the railway on one side and the road on the other. It too was made using Bath Stone but it was not of the best quality.

Mason's Mark

The stone is an excellent building material if seasoned before use, but doesn't weather well if used too soon after quarrying. The demand for stone became so great that the K&A Canal Company eventually opened its own quarry.

The aqueduct was finished in 1798 but the central arch began to sag almost immediately. It is now shored up with bricks which is not as attractive but is structurally safe. Grooves can be seen in the stone balustrade that have been worn by taught ropes pulling boats around the right-angle bends at each side of the valley.

Rope Marks

Avoncliffe Aqueduct passes over a road, the river and the railway.

This aqueduct, together with the Dundas Aqueduct, allows nine miles of lock free travelling ending at Bradford-on-Avon.

Avoncliffe Aqueduct

Bradford-on-Avon Wharf

BRADFORD-ON-AVON TO DEVIZES

It was in Bradford-on-Avon that the first turf of the canal was cut in 1794. The town's lock was the deepest before Locks 8 and 9 were merged to form Bath Deep Lock.

Next to it is a wharf area and some of the buildings still remain. There is also a former gauging dock where a boat's levels were measured for toll-collecting purposes. It is now a dry dock used for repairs and maintenance.

Between here and Devizes are

> There are five aqueducts between Bradford-on-Avon and Devizes.

five aqueducts, although none of them are as impressive as Dundas and Avoncliffe mentioned in the previous chapter. The first two can be found at Hilperton on the outskirts of Trowbridge. Both made of Bath Stone, the first crosses the River Biss while the other, Ladydown Aqueduct, passes over the railway. A little further on, Semington Brook is crossed by another with a single arch.

Near Buckley's Lock (15) is the site of the old Semington Junction. This is where the Wilts & Berks Canal joined the Kennet & Avon. The entrance is now bricked up but the stone house that doubled as a lock-keeper's cottage and a tollhouse can still be seen. Much of the Wilts & Berks is currently being restored but because the line of the canal between Semington and Melksham has been lost due to housing developments, there are plans for an alternative route, and a new junction will be created.

In 2004, major construction work was carried out to allow the canal to cross the new A350 bypass. This modern aqueduct is the first to have been built on the canal for two hundred years. It is made of concrete and is wide enough for two boats to pass. Although not as beautiful as the stone built ones of John Rennie, it is a reflection of today's engineering.

The five locks at Seend form a

New Aqueduct

flight that was dominated by an ironworks in Victorian times. It had three imposing blast furnaces each 15 metres (50ft) high and the canal played an important part in transporting the huge quantities of coal it needed to operate.

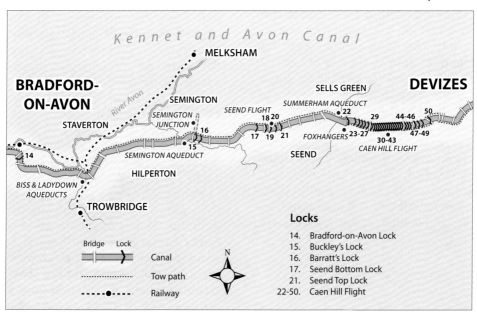

Kennet and Avon Canal

MELKSHAM

BRADFORD-ON-AVON

SEMINGTON

River Avon

STAVERTON

SEMINGTON JUNCTION

16

15

14

SEMINGTON AQUEDUCT

HILPERTON

BISS & LADYDOWN AQUEDUCTS

TROWBRIDGE

SEEND FLIGHT

18 20

17 19 21

SELLS GREEN

SUMMERHAM AQUEDUCT

22

FOXHANGERS

SEEND

29 44-46 50

23-27

30-43

47-49

CAEN HILL FLIGHT

DEVIZES

Bridge Lock

Canal

Tow path

Railway

N

Locks

14. Bradford-on-Avon Lock
15. Buckley's Lock
16. Barratt's Lock
17. Seend Bottom Lock
21. Seend Top Lock
22-50. Caen Hill Flight

Production stopped in 1889 when the furnaces were demolished. These days, there is little to suggest they ever existed.

Further on, the canal passes over the small Summerham Aqueduct before reaching Foxhangers' new marina.

This is where the steep climb of the Caen Hill flight begins, quite gently at first with seven locks. It is not until you emerge from under Upper Foxhangers Bridge that the full impact of the flight of sixteen closely grouped locks is seen. These are so close together that side ponds were created to store water for their use. Each one holds enough to fill the lock up to fourteen times. Electric pumps now return the used water to the top of the flight reducing

The K&AC Company had its own gasworks to provide lighting for the Caen Hill Locks at night.

concerns over the supply. The final six locks into the town of Devizes complete the rise of over 70 metres (237ft) in only two and a quarter miles.

This section was the last part to be finished. While the locks were under construction, the two halves of the canal were linked by a horse-drawn tramway.

Once the navigation was completed, the tramline became the towpath. This is why the path is so wide here and also why it has a separate archway under each of the road bridges.

Caen Hill Locks

Aerial View of Caen Hill Locks

The canal's economic peak came between the years of 1824 and 1839 and this was when the K&A Canal Company decided to make some improvements. One of them was installing gaslight at Caen Hill so the locks could be used at night. For the additional charge of a shilling for a barge or sixpence for a boat, they could be operated as long as the gas was lit. This was to help increase productivity which was especially welcome in the winter when daylight hours are reduced.

These days the locks may only be used during the daytime and it can take around five or six hours to negotiate the entire flight.

Devizes Wharf is home to The Kennet & Avon Canal Trust and Museum.

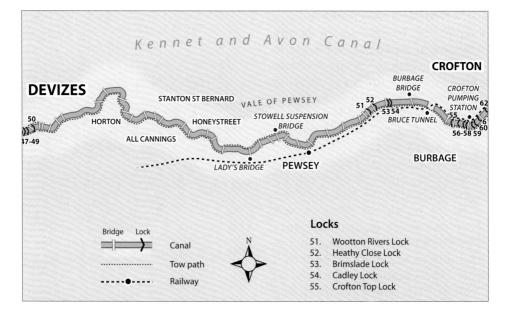

Locks

51. Wootton Rivers Lock
52. Heathy Close Lock
53. Brimslade Lock
54. Cadley Lock
55. Crofton Top Lock

DEVIZES TO CROFTON

After the dramatic rise at Caen Hill, the canal begins a fifteen-mile stretch without locks known as the Long Pound. It follows the contour of the land using embankment and cuttings to keep it level.

Leaving Devizes, there is a good view of the White Horse that was cut in 1999 to celebrate the turning of the millennium. The rolling chalk hills of the Pewsey Vale are perfect for this traditional art form. Another white horse can be seen at Alton Barnes from the canal near Honeystreet.

The success of Honeystreet Wharf was down to the owners Robbins, Lane & Pinniger who had one of the main boatbuilding companies on the canal. Although primarily boatbuilders and timber merchants, their business also included the manufacture of fertiliser, paint and cement which

were then distributed by their own fleet of boats. They owned most of the village and, being fairly enlightened for the time, offered their workers subsidised housing and even operated a sickness fund.

Many ancillary businesses grew up around the wharf to supply it. The pub was built to meet the needs of the increased traffic. The building provided a wide range of services including a general store, slaughterhouse, bakehouse, smokehouse and stabling as well as the brewery.

Before reaching Pewsey, there is a stone bridge that is different in style to the others. Ladies Bridge was built at the request of Lady Susannah Wroughton of Wilcot Manor as compensation for the canal cutting through her land. The K&A Canal Company agreed to build the ornamental bridge and to widen the canal to give the impression of a lake.

At Stowell Park, there is a suspension bridge which is the only one to cross the canal. Made of iron, its design is interestingly engineered with a tapering number of links.

The Long Pound finally comes to an end with four locks at Wootton Rivers. The last of these being Cadley Lock (54) which is sometimes known as Wootton Top Lock. Above these gates is the highest point of the canal therefore water is drained every time the lock at either end of the pound is used. More is fed into it from the pumping station at Crofton just above Crofton Top Lock (55) to keep it full.

Alton Barnes White Horse

A pound is the stretch of water between two locks.

At Burbage Wharf, near to the typical wharf-side building adjacent to the canal is a restored wharf crane. The work was

Ladies Bridge

carried out by the engineers at Claverton Pumping Station and was recently returned to its place at the canal side.

Immediately after is a good example of a skew bridge. The design was still being developed and this is one of the later versions of John Rennie's work.

The canal passes through a cutting before entering the Bruce Tunnel at Savernake Forest. Rennie's plans did not include a tunnel here as a deep cutting was the cheapest option. But the owner of the land, Thomas Bruce, insisted that it was built to hide the canal. It was the first of its kind on any canal network and required the ingenuity of Rennie to get it right.

Crofton Pumping Station still works on specified weekends and is operated by volunteers.

There is no towpath through it so before boats were motorised, they were hauled through the tunnel (459 metres; 502 yards) using a chain attached to the wall. Meanwhile, the horses were unharnessed and led over the top. It is said that the construction of the Caen Hill Locks was delayed because so many bricks were needed to complete the project.

The pumping station at Crofton was purpose-built in 1807 to supply water to the summit. Water is scarce on the chalk

Bruce Tunnel

Crofton Pumping Station

downland so a tributary of the River Dun has been dammed to form the lake Wilton Water opposite.

The steam-powered beam engines are capable of raising a ton of water (12 metres; 40ft) with each pump. This then flows along a feeder channel to the summit pound.

When, after 150 years, the chimney was found to be unsafe, it was partially dismantled. The engines could not work properly without sufficient draw and pumping ceased.

In 1968, the Kennet & Avon Canal Trust acquired the building and a group of retired engineers restored the two old beam engines to their former glory, one of which is now the oldest beam engine still capable of doing its job. Money was raised to rebuild the chimney to its original height and pumping was possible again.

Although the day to day work has been taken over by an electric pump, the old ones have been called back into action when the modern ones have broken down!

It is open for visitors during the summer and can be seen in steam on some weekends.

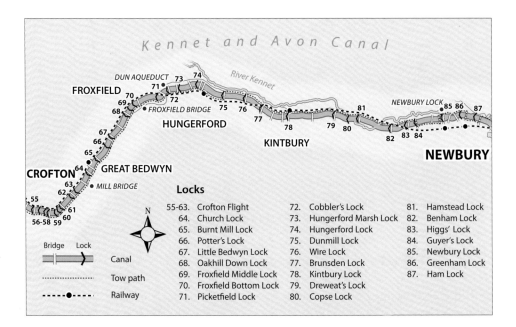

Kennet and Avon Canal

Locks

55-63. Crofton Flight	72. Cobbler's Lock	81. Hamstead Lock
64. Church Lock	73. Hungerford Marsh Lock	82. Benham Lock
65. Burnt Mill Lock	74. Hungerford Lock	83. Higgs' Lock
66. Potter's Lock	75. Dunmill Lock	84. Guyer's Lock
67. Little Bedwyn Lock	76. Wire Lock	85. Newbury Lock
68. Oakhill Down Lock	77. Brunsden Lock	86. Greenham Lock
69. Froxfield Middle Lock	78. Kintbury Lock	87. Ham Lock
70. Froxfield Bottom Lock	79. Dreweat's Lock	
71. Picketfield Lock	80. Copse Lock	

Bridge Lock

Canal

Tow path

Railway

CROFTON TO NEWBURY

Between the bottom of the Crofton Flight and Great Bedwyn is Mill Bridge which is thought to be the earliest example of a skew bridge. It is not a perfect specimen, but it clearly shows how these bridges evolved.

Bridges had always approached obstacles at right angles which often resulted in the road having dangerously sharp bends. This bridge was John Rennie's first attempt to 'iron out' those kinks by crossing the canal at a different angle. The design worked, but the brickwork was untidy. A later example with more regular brickwork is Burbage Bridge near the Bruce Tunnel mentioned in the previous chapter.

Great Bedwyn Wharf was once owned by the K&A Canal Company and served the surrounding agricultural area. Today, it is still a busy wharf with plenty of moorings. The village is home to Lloyd's stonemasons who were responsible for much of the work and maintenance on the eastern half of the canal including the Bruce Tunnel.

The River Dun can be seen between the canal and the railway at this point. Look out for the circular weir at Foxfield Bridge.

Approaching Hungerford, the canal crosses the river by the low three-arched brick Dun Aqueduct, and passes through a nature reserve where it is possible to see many wetland birds including herons and kingfishers. Reeds have been planted along this

Mill Bridge is
halfway between
Bath and Reading.

Traditional planting of
waterside plants helps
reduce erosion.

stretch, as they would have done when the canal was built, to reduce the effect of boat wash and now also to encourage water voles.

At Hungerford, the wharf-side building still exists but the wooden crane and timber piles have been replaced by a pleasant grassy bank.

Beyond the town, the River Kennet can be seen running near to the canal. This stretch of the river is designated as a Special Site of Scientific Interest, mainly because it is a chalk watercourse and supports rare plants and animals that can only live in its unique environment.

Circular Weir

Chalk was quarried in the area around Kintbury. It was transported to Bristol where it was washed and ground to be used in paint.

Between here and Hungerford during the summer months, it is

Dun Aqueduct

possible to take a trip on a barge hauled the traditional way by heavy horse and experience a flavour of times gone by. Horses are a very efficient method of pulling boats and even after the introduction of motorised craft they were still used commercially until the mid-twentieth century. It is now a tranquil and environmentally friendly way to enjoy a boat trip.

Newbury Lock (85) was the first to be built on the canal. To contrast the old with the new, the Town Council commissioned the sculptor Peter Randall-Page to create a modern work of art that would sit beside it. The result is a granite bowl that is designed to fill and empty at the same time as the lock. Called 'Ebb and Flow', it measures nearly 2½ metres (8ft) in diameter and is set in the centre of a spiral path. These two fascinating pieces of engineering in their own right have managed to create a positive link between the past and the present.

Just beyond is an attractive balustrade bridge which is one of the oldest over the canal. There is no towpath beneath it and horses were not allowed to haul across the bridge but instead had to be unharnessed. The towline was then floated underneath and reconnected to the horse on the other side. There was obviously some disregard for this rule as a

Horse-drawn Boat

Town Bridge, Newbury

a sign warning captains of a fine was put up at the lock.

In total, there were eighteen wharves in the vicinity of Newbury. The main one covered a huge area and was on the Reading side of the town. The site would have been unrecognisable 130 years ago with two large basins and a quay that could accommodate many barges. The basins were filled in and most of the buildings demolished in the early 1900s when they were no longer needed. The entrance was under the new road bridge and a restored crane has been erected as a reminder of the past. But as with many wharves these days, it is now used mainly as a car park.

Town Bridge was finished in 1769 before the middle section of the canal was cut.

KENNET & AVON CANAL
NOTICE
The Captain of every vessel allowing Horses to Haul across the Street will be Fined. *By Order*

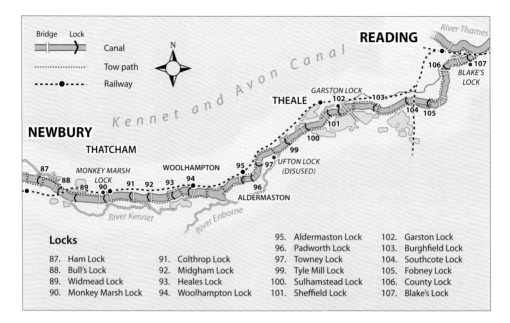

Locks

87. Ham Lock	91. Colthrop Lock	95. Aldermaston Lock	102. Garston Lock
88. Bull's Lock	92. Midgham Lock	96. Padworth Lock	103. Burghfield Lock
89. Widmead Lock	93. Heales Lock	97. Towney Lock	104. Southcote Lock
90. Monkey Marsh Lock	94. Woolhampton Lock	99. Tyle Mill Lock	105. Fobney Lock
		100. Sulhamstead Lock	106. County Lock
		101. Sheffield Lock	107. Blake's Lock

NEWBURY TO READING

Between Newbury and Reading, the course of the River Kennet is followed. The river, in its natural form, was unsuitable for navigation until the 1700s when new channels were cut to straighten meandering sections, and locks were built to overcome the gradient of the land.

At this time, all twenty locks were made with turf sides. The side 'walls' were earthed up to an angle of around 45 degrees and vegetation was encouraged to grow to keep them in place. Most have since been converted to brick with straight sides to reduce the amount of water used. Only

> **Early river locks were made with turf sides.**

two remain and they are both Grade II listed buildings. The first is Monkey Marsh Lock (90) near Thatcham and the other is Garston Lock (102) near Theale. Both these early river locks have steel rails to guide boats to the centre, which is especially important during a descent.

Aldermaston Lock's (95) turf sides were converted in the mid-eighteenth century and rebuilt with scalloped walls to the line of blue bricks. The attractive brickwork was extended to the top of the chamber during the restoration work in the 1980s. Just below the lock is a spur that was created as a connection between the canal and the railway. It is now greatly reduced and used for moorings.

The modern hydraulic lift bridge was also installed in the 1980s. It is controlled by boaters but restrictions don't allow it to be raised after dark or during peak traffic times.

Ufton Lock (98) was made redundant during the restoration. As the shallowest on the canal with a rise/fall of only ½ metre (1ft 9ins), it was thought that if the cut was deepened to the next lock it may not be needed. This was tried and was successful.

At Reading, there is a more urban landscape with a riverside development of shops and cafés. Here, even the boats are controlled by traffic lights because of dangerous bends and blind spots on the river.

In the centre of the town is High Bridge which is the oldest surviving bridge on the Kennet. It

High Bridge in Reading marks the official end of the canal.

also marks the administrative end of the canal, the last mile being under the control of the Thames Conservancy.

Reading was once known as 'biscuit town' because it was home to Huntley & Palmers' factory. Situated on the eastern side of the town, it relied on the canal to transport flour from local mills to the factory and smooth transportation of the finished biscuits to reduce breakages. Today, only the old recreation

Garston Lock

building can be seen near the canal but it still proudly wears the Huntley & Palmers' name.

In the thirteenth century, this stretch was the only part of the river that was navigable. The lock was a very basic flash lock which was an even earlier type of a river lock than the turf-sided ones. It worked by building up a head of water behind a small gate which would then be opened quickly and with the flash of water the boat would move downstream. To move upstream was more difficult because the boats needed to be winched through the small opening against the force of the water. It was originally known as Brokenborough Lock and came under the jurisdiction of the

Abbey. The abbot charged each boat a penny to pass through it.

Now called Blake's Lock (107), it is the last before the canal joins the Thames.

Blake's Lock